LETTS GUIDES TO
✧ GARDEN DESIGN ✧
Color

LETTS GUIDES TO
◆ GARDEN DESIGN ◆

Color

◆ DIANA SAVILLE ◆

CANOPY BOOKS
A Division of Abbeville Publishing Group
NEW YORK LONDON PARIS

First published in the United States in 1993
by Canopy Books, a division of Abbeville Publishing Group,
488 Madison Avenue
New York, NY 10022

First published in the United Kingdom in 1992
by Charles Letts & Co Ltd.
Letts of London House, Parkgate Road
London SW11 4NQ

Edited, designed and produced by Robert Ditchfield Ltd.
Copyright © Robert Ditchfield Ltd 1992.

ISBN 1 – 55859 – 551 – 1

A CIP catalog record for this book is available from the British Library.

ACKNOWLEDGEMENTS

Photographs are reproduced by kind permission of the following:
Deni Bown 61; Bob Gibbons 9, 15(above), 22, 26, 31, 36, 47,
58, 59 (all © Robert Ditchfield Ltd); W.A. Lord 13; Christine
Skelmersdale 60. All other photographs are by Diana Saville,
who would like to thank the owners of the gardens in which they
were taken, including Eastgrove Cottage Garden, Lower Hall,
Kellaways and The Priory.

ILLUSTRATIONS

Page 1: The white garden at Sissinghurst Castle.
Frontispiece: White *Persicaria paniculatum* above *Geranium
psilostemon.*
Page 5: *Paeonia arietina*

CONTENTS

INTRODUCTION

Colour is the single most important element in gardening design. It shapes borders and makes boundaries; it draws the eye to the distance and prevents it looking beyond the foreground; it disguises mistakes and embellishes assets. It stops and starts, compresses and elongates, antiques and modernizes.

There is little that colour cannot achieve, but it is much more than merely a design factor: it affects us too, for our response to colour is more sensitive than to form. We recognize the emotional force of particular hues, sharing the knowledge, part instinctive and part cultural, that green is a tranquilizer, red an agitator and yellow a symbol of cheerfulness. The gardener's response to white, however, shows how a cultivated response can override the traditional: although white symbolizes purity and innocence, a white garden has acquired the stamp of sophistication and chic, probably because of certain famous examples like the White Garden at Sissinghurst Castle. This is a 180 degree turn in our perceptions.

The successful use of colour in the garden therefore involves grasping a code of design, emotion and culture that can be more delicate than it might at first appear.

ABOVE: *Orange alstroemerias and red peonies are cooled by silver foliage.*
OPPOSITE: *Hot red crocosmias, yellow achilleas and solidagos reinforce one another.*

Factors that Affect Colour in the Garden

A gardener's colours will differ from an artist's. Colour in the garden is impure and unstable. An artist can predict the result of using precise quantities and shades of blue and pink oil paint in adjacent areas on a canvas. A gardener can plant his blue and pink flowers but knows that the weather (not just frost and rain, but wind and sun), the time of day, the degree of light, the temperature, the soil (acid or limy), the growth of the plants and even the colour instability that is inherent in many blossoms must all affect the success of the result.

All he or she can do is to take these variables into account by harnessing the environment to work to his advantage. Shade, sunlight, high and low pH factors of the soil (whether it is limy or acid) must all be used to bring out or diffuse the colour in some plants. In short, it is not sufficient, when making a colour garden, to be an artist-gardener. One has to be a good grower as well, armed with a sure knowledge of the tastes and habits of plants and of their simultaneous flowerings.

This last is most important. It would not present a challenge if you were dealing with only a few plants in a given season, but where you include clusters of plants in great variety, it demands some homework in advance. Colour combinations between plants can scarcely be planned until you establish their shared habits – when they flower, whether in sun or shade, and in what type of soil.

'Lavender Pinocchio', a cluster-flowered (floribunda) rose: its flowers change colour during their life-cycle.

The Effect of Sunlight

The colour of flowers is affected by the temperature, angle of the sun, the degree of cloud cover and by humidity. In the South – the Mediterranean, tropical Australia and certain southern states of America – the brilliance and clarity of light will greatly exceed that in Northern Europe. Intense light has a bleaching effect whereas cloud cover tends to enrich colours.

In practice this can present the gardener with a paradox. Because bright light bleaches, he or she knows that it would be unwise *from the point of view of colour* to plant a grey or silver border in brilliant sun. Its subtleties would be rendered void. But the gardener also knows that almost all grey and silver plants need full sun to thrive: grey and white leaves are there for the purpose of surviving heat and drought. A dilemma here? No, not so long as the gardener positions his grey border where he will only see it in the soft light of early morning or evening, a time which makes silvery foliage misty and luminous. Nor if, alternatively, he uses the grey leaves merely as a background to dominant crimson or intense violet flowers which he infiltrates into his scheme. Here, the pallor of the grey will have the effect of enriching its neighbours.

RIGHT: The China rose 'Mutabilis' has flaming buds and pale copper opening flowers which become pink and then soft crimson in maturity.

The Effect of Soil

Hydrangeas provide the best known example of the effect of soil on colour. Many cultivars will produce pink or crimson flowers in slightly alkaline soil (very alkaline is no good as the whole plant grows chlorotic), lilac in neutral soil, and intense gentian blue on the most acid soils. However, if you treat slightly alkaline or neutral soils, you can blue some varieties, chiefly *H. macrophylla* types. The usual method is to water them with a blueing compound, aluminium sulphate or alum, every ten days from bud break until flowering. The results can look crude so you might prefer to experiment with a weak solution or import acid compost for your plant.

With some other cases, there is no corrective you can apply. Autumn colouring of many trees, for example, will be greatly enriched on acid soil, but if your soil is unsuitable, there is little you can do to doctor it for so large a subject. The best way of ensuring rich seasonal effects is to select a tree clone whose colours are reliably good in autumn, regardless of the soil.

Temperature and Daylight

These factors can improve a plant's performance or ruin it, yet they are as beyond your influence as sunlight. All you can do is be aware of their effect and play safe or take risks with the plants you include. Many half-hardy subjects from tropical regions will simply fail to perform in a poor summer: the climbing Morning Glory (*Ipomoea rubro-caerulea*) for example, will scarcely get going. Others, such as the lovely chenille salvia which is grown from cuttings (*S. leucantha* with its velvety mauve tassels) are absolutely reliable, no matter what the weather.

On the other hand, ornamental cabbage – a brassica with pink or cream hearts which is sometimes grown as a decorative pot plant – will not produce its most intense colouring until night temperatures fall below 50°F/10°C and daylight hours reduce.

Knowing your Plants

The moral is to know your plants. This means knowing, too, which plants have unstable colouring. If you plant a gold border, for example, you might wish to know that the golden-leafed philadelphus, *P. coronarius aureus*, will turn green as the season advances. Or that *Rosa* 'Mutabilis' (you can't claim the name doesn't warn you) has flaming buds and copper-opening flowers which turn pink and then soft crimson in maturity. Or that the cluster-flowered rose 'Lavender Pinocchio' starts life as tan before its lavender-pink transformation.

Planning can only do so much, for you are dealing with living things which can be unpredictable. But then unpredictability is in itself one of the most addictive pleasures of gardening.

A late summer border of cool but rich colouring.

THE STUDY OF COLOR

The retina of the eye has colour receptors that respond to the wavelength of light, interpreted by the brain as colour. Appropriately, it was Sir Isaac Newton who conceived the first of all colour circles in the seventeenth century. It was based on his discernment that all colours were contained in the white light of the sun which was broken up when passing through a prism (as revealed in the rainbow). This spectrum ran from red through orange and into yellow, green, blue and indigo to violet. He recognized that, although the two extreme ends were red and violet, these two colours had a visual resemblance and, if mingled, produced a variety of purples 'such as are not like in appearance to any homogeneal light'.

The colour chart and its relevance to the arts were later explored in tremendous detail in Michel Chevreul's great 1854 treatise, *The Principles of Harmony and Contrast of Colours and their Application to the Arts.* Here he showed what he insisted were the three primaries, red, yellow and blue, so named because by mixing one or more in different proportions, all other colours can be produced. His chart showed his three binaries: orange, green and violet; and six intermediate colours: red-orange etc. His statements on colour harmony, summarized very briefly opposite, became the principles and laws of colour training thereafter, although some of his beliefs have been disputed by physicists and also by artists who take a far freer approach nowadays.

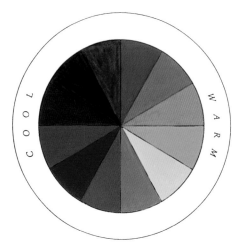

Michel Chevreul's colour circle.

Colour in the Garden

Nonetheless, many of his principles have remained valid and the division of the chart into warm and cool areas is used by gardeners as well as artists. A painter considers colours which approach orange, warm and fiery; those which tend to blues are cold. Warm tones added to other warm tones have an enhanced effect and remain luminous when mixed. But when warm and cool tones are mixed, the effect can be weakened. It is the problem for an artist to experiment with the colour tones in his picture to obtain the effect he needs. For a gardener the problem is the same, only he or she has infinitely more distractions and competition from his surroundings as I have already suggested.

A gardener, especially, is forced to take a less narrow and dogmatic approach to colour. Organic colours of animal or plant origin differ from inorganic or mineral pigments which form artist's colours. They are shifting and elusive, changed by the form of the flower (a mop-head blossom will intensify the hue, an airy umbel diffuse it) and changed too by the flower's texture.

In any case, the colours of flowers are so infinitely subtle and variable that they cannot be corseted into the simplification of a colour chart. Plantsman's charts are obtainable in the form of colour cards showing gradings of such minute variation that 808 shades are displayed to which flowers can theoretically be matched. I am not recommending these as a tool for the normal amateur gardener who would be an ass to angle for a flower to exemplify colour 174D. But they do enable the professional (and the pedant) to deal in specifics in so far as they can be relevant to gardening.

Michel Chevreul's Beliefs

Chevreul believed that:

i) tints and shades of the same hue make combinations of monochromatic harmony;

ii) neighbouring colours on the pure colour scale (the colour circle) are agreeable and he called this the harmony of adjacents;

iii) all colours gain in brilliance and purity by the proximity of grey (although he thought that grey and rose were a little dull, thereby rejecting a most cherished combination in today's gardens);

iv) triad combinations, such as black (for this, a gardener would substitute a very dark yew green), red and yellow were successful;

v) the proximity of complementary colours (i.e. the opposites on the colour circle such as blue and orange) were successful; also of split-complementary groups (i.e. the combination of a hue, not with its exact complementary, but with the two neighbouring colours that flank its complementary on the colour circle);

vi) if two colours combined badly, they could be separated by white, grey and, less relevantly to the gardener, black; this would make a neutral interval.

Jekyll-style twin borders of graded colour.

Gertrude Jekyll

Although the Impress-ionist artist Monet par-tially anticipated Gertrude Jekyll's lavish effects and use of colour in the garden, her exploration of its true poten-tial has never been equalled. Influenced by Chevreul and the Impressionists herself, and trained as a painter, a craft which failing eyesight in middle age had forced her to abandon, she applied her genius and obsessional per-fectionism to gardening.

Her views are apparent in most of her books, but her title *Colour Schemes for the Flower Garden* is the most detailed expression of her practice. Here she was concerned not only with the treatment of colour in individual flower borders, but with the sequence of its presentation throughout a (large) garden. She advised you to enter a gold garden from a shrub or tree plantation, sunshine after shade. The grey garden would be best reached through orange borders. From the grey garden you should proceed to the yellow, and thence to the blue garden (she was strict that only true blues should be used, save a couple of exceptions). And, from the blue garden, one progressed to the green area with its smattering of white flowers. I fear that the modern stroller with his three-second atten-tion span would be weary with exhaustion.

Moving from the general to the particular, her showpiece in her Munstead Wood home was her great hardy flower border, about 200ft/61m long and 14ft/4½m wide. Here, the two ends shared a groundwork of grey and glaucous foliage. At the western end, she massed and intermingled flowers of grey, grey-blue, white, palest yellow and palest pink. It then progressed to vivid yellows, orange and red, the 'strong and gorgeous' middle space, after which the colour receded in inverse sequence back through its spectrum, except at the eastern end where there were pure purples and lilacs instead of blues. The explanation for this was her aversion to mixing blues with purple and greyer blues, and only when the main mass of blue was over would she allow the presence of *Campanula lactiflora* or *Clematis heracleifolia* 'Davidiana'.

Monet's garden at Giverney, France, which he painted obsessively.

Jekyll's Inventiveness

In the course of her forty years as a garden designer, she planned more than 350 gardens, a quite prodigious output, and many of these were even more adventurous in their use of colour than her own garden at Munstead Wood.

She devised, for example, twin borders, not as parallels but as separated wings. One of these would be filled with flowers whose colours were drawn from the warm side of the spectrum. The other border would be planted with cool colours. This is a set-piece approach to colour which can still be seen in certain National Trust gardens in Britain, where a bright intense border is paired with one of muted and subtle colouring: at Cliveden in Surrey, at Tintinhull House in Somerset, and at Powis Castle in Wales.

It is a pity that Jekyll has become famous largely for the grandeur of her schemes where colour is orchestrated into crescendos. The attention she paid to intimate corners of gardens, to individual combinations was equally concerned and inventive, as the book, *Lost Gardens of Gertrude Jekyll* by Fenja Gunn, has demonstrated.

Autumnal gold and mauves but it is the white of the seat that dominates.

CREATING A COLOR BORDER

A ll the variables I have already sketched can make the creation of a colour border a daunting proposition. The simplest approach is to organize the process into stages.

The position of the colour border is the first matter for you to decide. This is crucial if you are to make the maximum use of its potential. Many colour borders are less flexible than the more casual mixed border since they usually rely heavily on herbaceous (and, often half-hardy annuals). Should you, for example, postion the border against a wall or plant an area within an enclosure if you have one? Or is it simpler to place your colour patch in the open, as in the case of twin beds lining a path? Or do you turn the whole of a tiny garden into a colour theme?

There is no doubt that enclosing the colour area is the easier option. If you position the border against a wall or limit the area's arena by a screen of dark hedges, you are excluding other visual disruptions to its impact. If you don't do this, you have the more difficult job of making it blend into its surroundings – or trying to harness them. This can be quite a challenge.

There is also another incentive for fully or partially enclosing a colour area. Namely, that an island bed or border is notoriously difficult to create since it must be equally presentable and varied to view on all four sides. This is very demanding when you have a limited palette. In any case, even the best island border which is seen broadside will give a poorer effect than a border or areas which are enfiladed. In the latter case, the colour is concentrated yet shown in perspective.

Colour in Context

Positioning also affects your colour, for where you choose may alter the hues you want. These cannot be imposed entirely at your will. Rather, the colour arises not only from the mood of the setting, but from its backcloth. Since a colour can be heightened or destroyed by its surroundings, you have to take into account whether the hues will harmonize with the brick, paint, houses, fields around them. Think, too, about the time of day you are likely to see the area. This is especially true with white and silver borders which are bleached in daylight, with blue or purple borders which fade quickly in evening light, with red which is oppressive on a hot day. Each colour has its characteristics, and these are outlined in the following section of the book.

Bands of harmonious colour organize these borders.

Close-up or Distance

You need to think, too, how colour will shape your garden. White flowers, for example, planted at the far-end of your area will jump forward and create a foreshortening effect. Light yellow, the most luminous of the colours, has the same ability to advance and meet the eye. Blue, on the other hand, will distance and elongate. The deeper purples, with their large admixture of black, will virtually disappear into the background if planted at a distance.

White Anthericum liliago and blush peonies are the last to fade at night. The rose is 'Cornelia'.

15

Sequence of Colour

Sequence of colour matters, too. I am not suggesting the kind of sequence proposed by Gertrude Jekyll (see page 12) which promotes a polychromatic odyssey. Simply, that if you have more than one colour area, which should come first? This was one of the issues explored in Michel Chevreul's great treatise, where he discussed the power of the after-image. His view was as follows: if you look at a blue square on a white ground, then fix your eye on the white, it will see orange. His explanation was that the retina, fatigued by blue, was disposed to receive a stronger impression of blue's complementary colour, orange. In the same way, you look for green after red.

This is important. At the famous garden of Hidcote Manor in Gloucestershire, the red borders are preceded by the green stage and followed by the green hornbeam alley. The sum of these is greater than its fine parts, and due in part to the arrangement of the colour sequence.

Composing the Scheme

Finally, after both position and colour of the bed are chosen, you can start to create the scheme. Perhaps the simplest approach is to list all the favourite shrubs and herbaceous plants in the range of colours you are selecting. Bear in mind their growth and form of flower before you include them, and be sure that they have shared tastes in soil, sunshine or shade.

Also, when choosing particular plants and their combinations, it is vital never to lose sight of plant habit. If this is ignored, you will end up with a solid wall of carpet-bedding, whereby flowers are reduced to one dimension only. Such a display has nothing to offer after its first glimpse, for colour is useless without good form too.

Assemble the plants into lists of simultaneous flowers. Star those which you want to feature in predominant groups – for when you are combining colours, you can't give equal weight to each colour, but should allow one to predominate, the rest to accent and flatter. Tick plants that are extra shapely. If you don't have enough with fine foliage or distinctive habit, add plants like plumy grasses whose leaves can be bright green, silver-variegated, blue, purplish or yellow. Eliminate the surplus and inferior plants. And then arrange your scheme as for a normal border, taking account of different heights and groupings, remembering that the latter will give you monochrome masses and should be scaled to context and partly intergrouped to prevent too solid colour blocks. The whole procedure can be summarized as merge, purge and splurge.

The Plant Lists

The following section of the book concentrates on individual colours and contains appropriate plant lists which range from dwarfs to trees in some cases. These lists are intended only to draw your attention to plants that are especially useful or beautiful individuals. Please note that plants, which may be the most frequently seen representatives of a colour, are often omitted. Key to flowering season: Sp = Spring; Su = Summer; A = Autumn; W = Winter; E = Early; L = Late. Also HHA = Half-hardy annual; E = Evergreen; T = Tender.

ABOVE: Colour in sequence: pink and red are impacted against green seen through the door, the latter cooling the former. Kolkwitzia amabilis 'Pink Cloud' is behind the rose 'Cerise Bouquet' on the left.

RIGHT: The red borders at Hidcote are preceded by the green stage and followed by green hedges.

White philadelphus and the rose 'Una' are warmed by pink alstroemerias.

THE WHITE GARDEN

White gardens are overwhelmingly the most popular of the colour areas, for they seem simple yet glamorous. The flowers look natural (nearly all common garden flowers have a white form) but, en masse, they have the sumptuousness of a bridal display. Such a garden represents the absolutes of purity and richness. A gardener who plans a white garden is therefore aiming for perfection as his or her target.

Perfection, however, is a tall order in gardening and in this case not easily attained. The simplicity of white gardens is deceptive. They represent a most sophisticated form of cultivation and one which is full of pitfalls for the novice. There must be more unsuccessful white gardens than of any other colour, because they are more challenging to execute and maintain. Failure is probable unless you consider two factors especially before planning a white area. The first is its position. The second is your choice of flowers, for you have to be even more discriminating about these than with any other colour garden.

WHITE SHRUBS

Abutilon vitifolium 'Album' E.Su.
Camellia 'Cornish Snow' Sp.
Carpenteria californica Su.
Cistus 'Elma' Su.
Hebe pinguifolia 'Pagei' Su.
Hibiscus syriacus 'Diana' L.Su. – A.
Hydrangea arborescens 'Annabelle' L.Su.
H. 'Lanarth White' L.Su.
Magnolia stellata 'Royal Star' Sp.
Paeonia suffruticosa 'Flight of Cranes' E.Su.
Philadelphus 'Sybille' Su.
Rhododendron 'Palestrina' (Azalea) Sp.
Romneya coulteri Su. – A.
Rose 'Iceberg' Su. – A.
Rosa rugosa alba Su. – A.
Rose 'White Wings' Su.
Viburnum plicatum 'Mariesii' E.Su.

WHITE ANNUALS

Argemone grandiflora
Cleome spinosa 'Helen
  Campbell' HHA
Lavatera trimestris 'Mont
  Blanc'
Nemophila maculata
Nicotiana affinis HHA
N. sylvestris HHA

BULBS

Anemone blanda 'White
  Splendour' Sp.
Crocus chrysanthus 'Snow
  Bunting' E.Sp.
Erythronium revolutum
  'White Beauty' Sp.
Fritillaria meleagris 'Alba'
  Sp.
Galtonia candicans L.Su.
Gladiolus colvillei 'The
  Bride' Su.
Lilium 'Olivia' L.Su.
L. regale Su.
L. speciosum 'Album'
  L.Su. - A.
Narcissus 'Mount Hood' Sp.
N. 'Thalia' Sp.
Trillium grandiflorum Sp.
Tulipa fosteriana
  'Purissima' (syn. 'White
  Emperor') Sp.
T. 'White Triumphator' Sp.

CLIMBERS

Clematis montana
  'Grandiflora' E.Su.
C. 'Huldine' Su. - A.
C. 'Mme. Le Coultre (syn.
  'Marie Boisselot') Su.
C. viticella 'Alba Luxurians'
  L. Su - A.
Hydrangea petiolaris Su.
Jasminum officinale Su.
Lathyrus latifolius 'White
  Pearl' Su.
Rose 'Climbing Iceberg'
  Su. - A.
Rose 'Paul's Lemon Pillar'
  Su.
Wisteria floribunda 'Alba'
  L.Sp
W. sinensis 'Alba' L.Sp.
W. venusta Sp.

A white seat flanked by Anthemis cupaniana.

Position

A white garden can only be fully effective if it is presented in its own area, preferably secret and enclosed. A dark surrounding formal hedge is perhaps the ideal, because it will not only limit the arena but intensify the impact. But a fence clothed with deep green ivy will provide as effective a contrast to a white garden as any hedge and is also less demanding to maintain.

Securing the right background to white flowers is only part of the story. What is overhead matters as well, by which I mean the light. One has to remember that white flowers are far from their best in strong daylight, which can bleach the differences in shades of white, pastels and pale-coloured leaves. They look far lovelier instead at dusk. In ancient Hindu gardens, this truth was utilized in an extreme form, for white-flowered Indian gardens were actually designed to be seen at night when they would gleam like phosphorescence under the moon. They would have also smelt at their sweetest at this hour, for many white flowers are inebriatingly fragrant. A white garden that is planned with this in mind can offer a most sensuous experience to the gardener.

ABOVE: Note how the violets in this kind of perspective act as shadows, giving depth to the whites.

LEFT: Cistus aguilari 'Maculatus'. This has a shorter flowering season than most cistus but is nonetheless one of the most spectacular.

Choice of flowers

Here one has to be very discriminating indeed for it is vital to assess not only the appearance of the flower but its manner of dying. The best white flowers for your purpose are those that shatter cleanly when they die. The worst are those that darken lingeringly – buddlejas are in the forefront of offenders – in which case your white garden may become famous for becoming your brown garden.

Blending Colours with White

White varies like any other colour. Some flowers are milk white, others have a faint blush, whilst many are creamy or buttery. The gardener who takes the chance to reinforce these variations will build a much more interesting area than the purist who adheres grimly to laundry white. A garden that has emerged from the detergent packet is very dull. So is a garden which relies only on densely white flowers which will produce a solid wall-to-wall carpet. Use the gauzy whites of crambe and gypsophila, which introduce air-pockets into your scheme. See-through white is more romantic than solid white.

Foliage Plants

Foliage plants will emphasize the range and depth of shadows. Deep greens will act as a foil. Greys and silvers will help it shimmer. Cream-and-green variegated leaves are sometimes favoured, but their 'fuss' can detract from the rich simplicity of a scheme. Restfulness rather than distraction is what one seeks in a white area. Many white-flowered plants have excellent grey and silver leaves themselves, and offer dual value to the garden.

WHITE PERENNIALS

Agapanthus campanulatus albus L.Su.
Anemone 'Honorine Jobert' L.Su. – A.
Campanula latiloba alba Su.
C. persicifolia alba Su.
Cimicifuga simplex 'Elstead' A.
Crambe maritima Su.
Dianthus 'Charles Musgrave' Su.
Dicentra spectabilis alba Sp.

Digitalis purpurea alba Su.
Geranium clarkei 'Kashmir White' Su.
Helleborus orientalis Sp.
Hosta 'Royal Standard' L.Su.
Iris sibirica 'White Swirl' E.Su.
Lychnis coronaria 'Alba' Su.
Malva moschata 'Alba' Su.
Paeonia 'White Wings' E.Su.
Papaver orientale 'Black and White' E.Su.
Primula japonica 'Postford White' E.Su.

Pulmonaria officinalis 'Sissinghurst White' Sp.
Viola cornuta 'Alba' Su. – A.
Yucca filamentosa L.Su.

TREES

Eucryphia nymansensis 'Nymansay' L.Sp.
Magnolia × soulangeana 'Alba' Sp.
M. salicifolia Sp.
Malus hupehensis Sp.
Prunus 'Shirotae' ('Mt. Fuji') Sp.
P. 'Tai Haku' Sp.

The *acid-yellow of* Alchemilla mollis *sharpens the blue* Agapanthus *'Headbourne Hybrids'.*

THE BLUE GARDEN

Blue behaves in the opposite way from white. It is a recessive colour, the last to assert itself at dawn and the first to fade at dusk. Its mistier shades will give the effect of distance if planted towards the rear of a border or the back of a garden. Designers have long exploited this characteristic to convey the impression that a border or garden is longer than in reality. This works, but only if the border is viewed *enfilade* and if the border or garden is a reasonable length anyway.

The cyanic colours, as blues are known, are often unstable on different soils but will take strong sunlight without dazzling the onlooker or bleaching. Another of their advantages in the garden is that many blue blossoms flower late in the season enabling you to mingle them with the softer mauves of the autumnal asters. Gertrude Jekyll was strict in her separation of true blues from purple-blues, considering that a pure palette offered greater beauty than a mingled one in this respect. This is less true of the softer tints. Mingling these has the subtle effect of shot silk, and a border of soft blues grading towards purples is both soothing and rich.

BLUE ANNUALS

Consolida orientalis (larkspur)
Ipomoea purpurea (Morning Glory) HHA
Nemophila menziesii
Nigella damascena
Phacelia campanularia
Salvia patens HHA

BULBS

Chionodoxa luciliae Sp.
Iris reticulata 'Cantab'
Muscari armeniacum Sp.
Scilla peruviana Su.
Scilla sibirica 'Spring Beauty'

PERENNIALS

Agapanthus campanulatus 'Isis' L.Su.
A. 'Headbourne Hybrids' Su.
Anchusa italica 'Loddon Royalist' Su.
Brunnera macrophylla Sp.
Campanula carpatica Su.
C. cochlearifolia Su.
C. persicifolia Su.
Clematis heracleifolia 'Wyevale' L.Su.
Convolvulus sabatius Su. – A.
Delphinium 'Black Knight' (dark) Su.
D. 'Loch Leven' (pale) Su.
Eryngium alpinum Su.
Gentiana asclepiadea L.Su. – A.
G. septemfida L.Su.
Iris sibirica 'Flight of Butterflies' Su.
Linum perenne Su.
Meconopsis grandis E.Su.
Omphalodes verna Sp.
Phlox bifida 'Blue' Sp.
Platycodon grandiflorus 'Mariesii' Su.
Polemonium foliosissimum Su.
Pulmonaria angustifolia 'Munstead Blue' Sp.
Salvia haematodes Su.
S. uliginosa A.
Veronica incana Su.

Blue delphiniums flank the yellow rose 'Graham Thomas' (one of Chevreul's split-complementary harmonies).

Other Blue Combinations

Blue on its own can look dull. Unlike whites which sing out against the greens of a garden's framework, blue and green are of insufficient contrast. Blue needs instead a touch of its chromatic near-opposite, yellow, to bring it definition. One of the most delicate and lovely combinations I have seen was in a bed of *Meconopsis grandis* (the Himalayan Blue Poppy), interplanted with the soft lime-yellow biennial *Smyrnium perfoliatum*. The same impression could be achieved with a range of euphorbias among blues. Their bracts hold their bitter lemon colour for so long, spring to early summer, that they could be partners for a succession of blue flowers.

One is not confined, of course, to partnering just blossom. The clouds of blue flowers spraying above *Brunnera macrophylla* look enchanting beside Bowles' Golden Grass (*Millium effusum* 'Aureum'). Or the golden yellow foliage of the invasive Creeping Jenny (*Lysimachia nummularia* 'Aurea') could form a groundwork for the blue butterflies of *Viola* 'Boughton Blue' or other pale blue cultivars.

Blue is a colour that is noticeably absent from certain groups of favourite garden plants, of which roses are the most significant. (One cannot consider attempts at blue roses to be any more than flights of imagination.) A garden without roses is deprived of choice and scent. If you introduce roses, you are therefore committing yourself to breaking up the blue mass – a decision which is probably to the garden's advantage. Again, soft yellows are beautiful with blues, such as the shrub rose 'Canary Bird' with its small single flowers and ferny leaves; or the bush rose 'Graham Thomas' (double, fragrant) which flowers throughout summer and autumn and can therefore accompany a succession of blue blossoms.

Variety in the Blue Garden

Often the same flower is obtainable in both blue and white – as with gentians, campanulas, geraniums, delphiniums and agapanthus, to name the most common. A successful way to use the same flower in two colours is to choose one with a pronounced outline: repeated planting will therefore look confident rather than thoughtless. Blue and white geraniums are confusing together, neither strong enough to hold its own against the other, yet insufficiently harmonious to blend. However, the photograph on this page shows how agapanthus retain their statuesque independence but blend through the uniformity of outline. The interchanging colours also save the line of plants from the charge of monotony.

Ceanothus

Blue flowers are mostly deficient in perfume, but the great exception is ceanothus. A huge bush will scent the air for yards with the sweet honey fragrance of its flowers. These shrubs are the backbone of the blue garden. Many are tender to harsh frost and must be planted against a wall in colder regions, but they are indispensable. A large garden should be packed with them for blue waves in spring and again in late summer if a range of varieties is planted. The small or average garden cannot spare the space, but they make excellent hosts for climbing plants (such as the late-flowering clematis). The spring-blooming ceanothus make good rent-payers if used for this secondary purpose in their off-season.

Ceanothus also attract bees, and so do many blue flowers. To a few unlucky people, this could be a disadvantage. To me it is a pleasure. The blue garden hums with life; it is part of a larger natural world and an illustration of the fact that a choice of colour has more than merely an aesthetic impact.

SHRUBS	
Caryopteris × *clandonensis* 'Kew Blue' L.Su. – A.	'Topaz' (indigo; T)
Ceanothus (Sp.-flowering) E	*Hydrangea* 'Blue Bird' Su. – A.
C. arboreus 'Trewithen Blue' T	H. 'Blue Wave' A.
C. 'Cascade'	*Lithodora diffusa* Sp. onwards
C. 'Delight'	*Perovskia atriplicifolia* 'Blue Spire' L. Su. – A.
C. 'Puget's Blue'	*Rosmarinus* 'Severn Sea' Sp.
C. thyrsiflorus repens	
Ceanothus (A.-flowering) E	
C. 'Autumnal Blue'	CLIMBERS
C. 'Burkwoodii'	
Ceanothus (Su. – A., deciduous)	*Clematis* 'Perle d'Azur' L.Su. – A.
'Gloire de Versailles'	*C.* × *durandii* (indigo) Su.
	Passiflora caerulea Su. – A.

The hybrid perpetual rose 'Reine des Violettes'.

THE PURPLE GARDEN

PURPLE ANNUALS

Brachychome 'Purple Splendour' HHA
Cleome 'Violet Queen' HHA
Cobaea scandens HHA
Heliotropium 'Marine' HHA
Lathyrus odoratus 'North Shore' (Sweet Pea)
Petunia 'Plum Purple' HHA
Viola 'Bowles Black'

BULBS

Allium aflatunense E.Su.
A.a. 'Purple Sensation' E.Su.
A. christophii Su.
A. giganteum Su.
Crocus speciosus A.
C. tommasinianus 'Whitewell Purple' Sp.
Iris reticulata Sp.
Tulip 'First Lady' Sp.
Tulip 'Negrita' Sp.

A gardener needs to interpret purple liberally to include neighbouring shades and tints. For one reason, true purple is the colour associated with ceremony and also with suffering, bizarrely at odds with a garden. Purple may be a rare sign of mourning nowadays, but old associations leave lingering impressions and can induce a feeling of unease whose origin is long since forgotten.

In any case, a relaxed interpretation of the colour is necessary because many of the so-called blue flowers have a lavender cast to their blooms. Intense magentas are also numerous, whether in wild or garden forms. This deviance from true purple also exists at the dark end of the scale: many purple leaves, for example, which form much of the background colour in this kind of border, aren't actually purple for much of their life. Purple foliage may unfurl in ruby tints, before acquiring the muddy hues of black pudding. Alternatively, the leaves of some plants spend much of their early weeks, even months, green until their transformation.

All these variations are actually of great advantage to the purple border which would be stolid and depressing without them. It needs leavening and the infiltration of brighter or paler colours is one method. There is another device and that is to position your purples with care.

26

Season

Purple is glamorously represented at all seasons from tulips, violets, wisteria in spring, to irises in summer, but perhaps it is at its most useful in subsequent months as it is a good late developer. Autumn can last for three months in full flower if you concentrate on the main violet flowers at the end of the year: notably asters and scarlet and purple fuchsias. These head the ranks of some of the longest blossoming flowers that we have. They include front-row sprawlers like verbena, and middle-rank bedders such as penstemons (there are several violet cultivars). You can add, too, the more corpulent shrubs like hebes and buddlejas and a late-flowering backcloth of clematis – not only the ubiquitous velvety 'Jack-manii' but the dusky C. *viticella*, an admirable choice since it is resistant to wilt.

You can also include some of the most ravishing half-hardy climbers: *Cobaea scandens* which will cover yards of wall or pergola with its large purple cups. Or *Asarina* (syn. *Maurandia*) *scandens* which is less vigorous but has showers of small intensely violet trumpets. Or *Rhodochiton volubile*, a curious beauty with a purple tube and deep rose calyx, makes a third. However, the colour all these provide can come very late in a cool season.

Abutilon × suntense *and* Erysimum *'Bowles' Mauve' lit by a background sun.*

Position

Never place your purples in deep shade which will make them seem dead and dreary. Better yet, try to position them so that the sun is behind them for that part of the day when you are most likely to see them. Sun through dark purple leaves and flowers electrifies them into life, makes them glitter like bronze. The third rule is a prohibition for country gardeners. Be wary of placing your purples at the edge of the garden, for they never look natural or comfortable when viewed against green fields and trees.

ABOVE: *Soft mauve and purple dominated border with* Allium aflatunense, violas, Thalictrum aquilegifolium *and pink peonies.*

LEFT: *A range of mauves:* magenta *Geranium psilostemon, blue-violet* G. 'Johnson's Blue', *lilac* Thalictrum aquilegifolium, *drawn together by silver or glaucous foliage.*

PURPLE CLIMBERS

Clematis 'Barbara Jackman'
 E.Su.
C. 'Gipsy Queen' L.Su. – A.
C. 'Jackmanii' L.Su. – A.
C. viticella 'Purpurea Plena
 Elegans'L.Su. – A.
C. 'Vyvyan Pennell' Su.
Solanum crispum
 'Glasnevin' Su. – A.
Wisteria floribunda L.Sp.
W.f. 'Macrobotrys' L.Sp.
W.f. 'Violacea Plena' L.Sp.
W. sinensis L.Sp.

Structure

One distinctive use of purple is to plan it into the structure of the garden. You might favour the soft floriferous edging of the herbaceous *Nepeta* × *faassenii* or prefer the shrubbier lines of lavender, whether the low, sharply violet *L. angustifolia* 'Hidcote' or the bosomy *L.* 'Grappenhall' which has paler flowers. Both kinds will form a scented framework.

You can also incorporate herbs and vegetables into the violet garden which will informalize it. Try the purple basil (*Ocimum basilicum* 'Dark Opal'), or chives with their small mauve domes. Or globe artichokes if you are willing to forgo the pleasures of eating them. These tall handsome perennials with their grey leaves and fringed violet flowers will perform the function of natural statues here. The self-seeding biennial *Onopordon arabicum* with its flauntingly silver spiny leaves will have much the same effect though its inedible violet heads are less spectacular.

Regardless of the flowers they sport, silver-leafed plants will freshen the purple border. Put carpets of *Artemisia schmidtiana* 'Nana' with its silver fur, beside violet pansies. Or shower mauve starry sisyrinchiums near the glaucous ground-cover of *Acaena* 'Blue Haze'.

Please see page 45 for plants with purple foliage.

PURPLE PERENNIALS

Aster × *frikartii* L.Su. – A.
A. sedifolius A.
A. thomsonii 'Nana' L.Su.
Campanula glomerata
 'Superba' E.Su.
C. portenschlagiana (syn. *C. muralis*) Su.
Geranium magnificum (syn. *G. ibericum*) Su.
G. psilostemon (magenta) Su.
Iris chrysographes Su.
I. germanica 'Braithwaite' Su.
I. kaempferi (syn. *I. ensata*) Su.
Limonium latifolium
 'Violetta' L.Su.
Liriope muscari A.
Malva sylvestris mauritiana Su.
Nepeta × *faassenii* Su.
Origanum laevigatum
 L.Su. – A.
Penstemon 'Stapleford Gem' L.Su. – A.
Pulsatilla vulgaris Sp.
Roscoea purpurea Su.
Salvia × *superba* 'East Friesland' Su.
Sisyrinchium bermudianum Su.
Stachys macrantha Su.
Viola cornuta Su. – A.
V. labradorica purpurea Sp.
V. odorata 'Princess of Wales' Sp.

SHRUBS

Buddleja alternifolia E.Su.
B. davidii 'Black Knight' L.Su.
Fuchsia 'Margaret'
 L.Su. – A.
Hebe speciosa 'Alicia Amherst' L.Su.
H.s. 'Purple Queen' L.Su.
Hydrangea villosa L.Su.
Lavandula angustifolia
 'Hidcote' Su.
L.a. 'Grappenhall' Su.
L. stoechas E.Su.
Syringa 'Elinor' E.Su.
S. × *persica* E.Su.

LEFT: Camellia *'Waterlily'*.

THE PINK AND PASTEL GARDEN

Pinks and related pastels – lilacs, lavenders, salmons – are tints: pale versions of purple or red with a varying admixture of white. Even in a single flower, a range of these tones can be present, as in some of the most glorious Gallica roses, whether in the crazy flaking and striping of 'Camaieux' or the graded extravagance of 'Président de Sèze' which has a crimson-purple heart, fading through lilac and pink to blush at the rim of its petals.

This curious distinction is not confined to roses. Other pink or lilac flowers have dark centres, such as *Cosmos* 'Daydream', or the tender shrub *Lavatera maritima bicolor*; and this arty visual coding (actually a prosaic device for directing insects) runs through many different and beautiful species.

Blendings of this kind point the way to a most effective use of pink in a garden, where it can be associated with the richest of deep crimsons and the purest of glistening whites – an extension of the harmony that can be apparent in a single flower. It is the reason why a planting of mixed old roses is unfailingly sympathetic.

Opalescence is another quality of many pink flowers, for their petals hover between lilacs and blues. Penstemons like *P.* 'Mother of Pearl', or *P. glaber*, or *Phlox* 'Mother of Pearl' all share this nacreous quality. Again, one can separate out these colours and combine pinks with blues and purples, the neighbouring shades in the spectrum, to make a restful scheme. Too restful? Perhaps, if you eschew the darker shades and add a preponderance of silver leaves. No, if you give it the ballast of strong tones and infiltrate deep green or purple foliage.

By now it will have become apparent that pink on its own can make a garden die of anaemia. Being neither one thing (crimson) nor the other (white), its application needs a firm hand.

PINK AND PASTEL PERENNIALS

Androsace lanuginosa Su.
Anemone × *hybrida*
 'Hadspen Abundance'
 L.Su. – A.
A. 'Queen Charlotte'
 L.Su. – A.
Astilbe 'Amethyst' Su.
Dianthus 'Pike's Pink' Su.
Diascia elegans Su. – A.
Dicentra eximia 'Stuart
 Boothman' E.Su.
Dierama pulcherrimum Su.
Erodium macradenum Su.
Geranium cinereum
 'Ballerina' Su.
G. macrorrhizum
 'Ingwersen's Variety' Su.
G. 'Mrs Kendall Clarke'
 (lilac) Su.
G. sanguineum
 lancastriense Su.
Gypsophila 'Rosy Veil'
 L.Su.
Helianthemum 'Wisley
 Pink' Su.
Hemerocallis 'Catherine
 Woodbury' Su.
H. 'Pink Damask' Su.
Hosta 'Kroussa Regal'
 (lavender) Su.
Lamium maculatum 'Beacon
 Silver' E.Su.
Paeonia 'Bowl of Beauty'
 Su.
P. 'Mons. Jules Elie' Su.
Papaver orientalis 'Cedric
 Morris' E.Su.
P.o. 'Mrs Perry' E.Su.
Penstemon glaber Su.
P. 'Mother of Pearl' Su. – A.
Phlox 'Mother of Pearl'
 L.Su.
Schizostylis 'Sunrise' A.
Sidalcea 'Rose Queen' Su.
Tradescantia ×
 andersoniana 'Pauline'
 Su.

Two very rare roses: 'Le Rire Niais' (foreground) and the Gallica 'Bellard'.

Warm and Cool Pinks

Pink has another quality that can be exploited. Its place within the spectrum is at that turning-point where the cool side merges with the warm: for pink can be a tint of crimson which contains blue, or a tint of vermilion which has a yellow content. If the latter, the pink is salmon, a colour not at all to my taste, though it is currently fashionable. The two pinks are not necessarily at variance and many flowers contain both tints, such as the hybrid musk rose 'Cornelia'. Again, if you separate out these shades in your garden (that is, into blue, pink, salmon and lemon), you can create a harmonious whole. But your message will be mixed for you are merging warm with cool.

PINK ANNUALS

Cosmos 'Daydream' HHA
Lavatera trimestris 'Pink Beauty'
Nigella 'Persian Jewels' (mauve, rose, white, blue)
Oenothera albicaulis HHA (white/pink)
Papaver rhoeas 'Mother of Pearl'
Saponaria vicaria 'Alba'

BULBS

Allium oreophilum (*A. ostrowskianum*) Su.
Amaryllis belladonna A.
Anemone blanda 'Pink Star' Sp.
Crinum × *powelli* L.Su.
Cyclamen hederifolium A.
Lilium 'Pink Perfection' Su.
L. tigrinum 'Pink' Su.
Nerine bowdenii A.
Tulip (lily-flowering) 'China Pink' Sp.

LEFT: *Japanese anemones are the pink mainstay for late summer onwards.*
OPPOSITE: *Deep pink with white: the Bourbon rose 'Mme Isaac Pereire' and 'Una'.*

Pink through the Seasons

One of the great assets of this colour is that the most beautiful and seasonally indispensable groups of plants are obtainable in a variety of pinks. One chooses from camellias in spring, peonies in early summer, pinks (dianthus) themselves and roses in high summer, anemones in autumn followed by nerines at the end of the year. These plants are such abundant flowerers and many so generous in their fragrance, that a garden can be distinguished by a preponderance of these varieties.

Although all make a show at a distance, many of these flowers are also characterized by the kind of detailing that invites the closest scrutiny. Just think of the slender *Camellia* 'E.G. Waterhouse', pale pink and the possessor of a formal double blossom, the most perfect of all known flower arrangements with row upon imbricated row of curving petals, mathematically spaced. Or of the maroon-laced pink, 'London Delight'. Or the luxuriant heads of a Bourbon rose like 'Souvenir de la Malmaison' with its quartering of pale tissued petals. Plants which catch the attention from both nearby and faraway make a desirable garden.

PINK SHRUBS

Camellia 'E.G. Waterhouse' Sp.
C. 'Elsie Jury' Sp.
C. 'Leonard Messel' Sp.
Cistus 'Silver Pink' Su.
C. 'Peggy Sannons' Su.
Daphne cneorum 'Eximia' L.Sp.
D. x *burkwoodii* ('Somerset') L.Sp.
Deutzia 'Rosalind' Su.
Hydrangea 'Preziosa' L.Su. - A.
Kolkwitzia amabilis 'Pink Cloud' Su.
Lavatera 'Barnsley' L.Su. - A.
Magnolia x *loebneri* 'Leonard Messel' Sp.
Paeonia suffruticosa 'Lord Selborne' E. Su.
Prunus tenella 'Fire Hill' Sp.
Rhododendron yakushimanum Sp.
Robinia hispida 'Rosea' Su.
Rosa x *alba* 'Celestial' Su.
R. 'Dearest' Su.
R. 'Felicia' Su.
R. 'Fritz Nobis' Su.
Syringa x *josiflexa* 'Bellicent' L.Sp.
Viburnum x *bodnantense* 'Dawn' A. - W.

V. x *juddii* Sp.
Weigela flórida 'Foliis Purpureis' Su.

CLIMBERS

Clematis 'Comtesse de Bouchaud' L.Su. - A.
C. 'Hagley Hybrid' L.Su.
C. *macropetala* 'Markham's Pink' Sp.
C. *montana* 'Tetrarose' Sp.
C. 'Nelly Moser' E.Su.
C. *texensis* 'Etoile Rose' L.Su. - A.
Rose 'Albertine' Su.
R. 'Débutante' Su.
R. 'Mme Caroline Testout' Su.
R. 'Mme Grégoire Staechelin' E.Su.
R. 'New Dawn' Su.

TREES

Crataegus oxycantha 'Rosea Flore Pleno' L.Sp.
Magnolia 'Heaven Sent' Sp.
M. 'Picture' Sp.
Malus floribunda L.Sp.
M. 'Pink Perfection' L.Sp.
Prunus 'Accolade' Sp.
P. x *blireana* Sp.
P. *subhirtella* 'Autumnalis Rosea' A. - Sp.

The power of a red and purple border with dahlias, lobelias, nicotianas and purple-leafed Cotinus coggygria.

THE RED GARDEN

R ed, like its tint of pink, is at the turning-point of the spectrum where the cool and the warm sides join. 'Cool' reds are the rubies and garnets: in practical terms, they range from the cerise pinks of cistus and down to the deep, sumptuous maroons of peonies and velvety old roses. Of all colours, these provide opulence in the border, undimmed in sunshine, glowing in shade where the flowers will tolerate it.

'Hot' reds, the scarlets and vermilions with their yellow content, are less easy to place. These emphatic, fiery colours can easily appear strident; and, unlike the crimsons, they cannot be cooled down with grey foliage which conflicts with their colour. Yet green, their chromatic opposite, only underlines their brilliance. In a large garden and used occasionally, their brightness can be more easily absorbed but, in a small area, it is wise to ponder whether you can live with their power.

RED ANNUALS   (H = hot red)

Antirrhinum 'Black Prince' HHA
Eschscholzia 'Cherry Ripe'
Godetia 'Firelight'
Helianthus 'Velvet Queen'
Linum rubrum
Nasturtium 'Empress of India'
Papaver commutatum 'Lady Bird' H

BULBS

Anemone fulgens H: Sp.
Crocosmia masonorum H: L.Su.
Dahlia 'Bishop of Llandaff' H: L.Su. – A.
D. 'Grenadier' H: L.Su. – A.
D. purpurea laciniata L.Su. – A.
Gladiolus byzantinus Su.
Lilium 'Journey's End' Su.
L. speciosum rubrum L.Su. – A.
Schizostylis coccinea 'Major' A.
Tulipa fosteriana 'Cantata' H: Sp.
T.f. 'Red Emperor' ('Mme. Lefeber') H: Sp.
T. greigii 'Red Riding Hood' H: Sp.
T. 'Queen of Sheba' (lily-flowering) H: Sp.
T. sprengeri H: L.Sp.

Using Reds

The brilliance of scarlets and the brighter reds means that they act as accents; they advance, attracting the eye to themselves or to whatever you wish to emphasize beside them. This attribute has its disadvantages. If the reds are placed at regular intervals along a border, the eye will tend to bounce along their line. By the second or third block of colour, tedium will have set in.

Two precautions will help to avoid this. First, it is wise to avoid regular placing of bright reds. Second, their effect can be modified if they are accompanied by plants drawn from the neighbouring shades on the spectrum. This has the effect of increasing their range, endowing them with a subtlety which they lack on their own. It is why purple and apricot are often introduced in a red border, the former deepening and cooling the reds, the latter lifting and warming them.

Antique and Modern Effects

The cool and hot reds are distinguished not only by their colour values: they can have the additional effect of placing a garden in a different context. The cool reds tend to give an antique appearance to a garden, for these are the colours of many old peonies, roses and dianthus. The scarlets, in contrast, can modernize: think of crocosmias and numerous modern roses which have been bred with yellow in their make-up. This colour language is not absolute but indirect, varying with the plants one chooses to include, for there are some old scarlet peonies and also modern purple-crimson roses, though these are usually bred to ape ancestral cultivars.

Modification by Foliage

One can also use foliage to modify reds. Grey-leafed plants, whether artemisias, the silvery *Stachys byzantina*, blue rues or steely grasses, frequently partner the crimsons and carmines. Their smoky shades bring out the blues in these reds and form some of the finest plant combinations.

Purple foliage is the other favourite to accompany reds. It has the effect of adding ballast to the brilliant reds, and its dullness subdues their show. An entire border composed of red flowers and purple foliage will always seem a contrived though spectacular arrangement but the occasional blended introduction adds a more natural note of gaiety. After all, a number of red-flowered plants are purple-leafed anyway – a few tender cannas, forms of *Lobelia cardinalis*, and some of the most elegant dahlias, notably *D*. 'Bishop of Llandaff'.

Dahlia laciniata purpurea.

OPPOSITE: *The rambler rose 'Bleu Magenta', though scentless, is the most sumptuous of the dark blue-purple-reds.*
LEFT: *The Gallica rose 'Charles de Mills', its velvet purple-crimson intensified by the pinks beside it.*

Seasonal Change

Red is not a colour one spontaneously associates with spring, yet it includes some of the finest tulips, like a few early-flowering *T. fosteriana* hybrids, the later lily-flowered 'Queen of Sheba' and, the last of all to bloom, *T. sprengeri*. But it seems perverse to have massed reds in spring: better to allow these as occasional notes, unless they are given their own exotic area.

The cool reds – burgundy, crimson, blue-pink – are for summer. In green shade (plants such as *Primula japonica* 'Miller's Crimson' or 'Valley Red' enjoy these conditions), they will glow like jewels. In full sun, the cool reds are mostly stable enough to hold their colour, though roses tend to turn purplish. This has its advantages as, unlike the vermilions, they will not increase the oppression of a hot day.

It is, however, in autumn that the scarlets come into their own. When the leaves turn part gold and red, it is now that vermilion flowers take their natural place in the landscape and seem less of an imposition.

RED PERENNIALS

Aster novi-belgii 'Winston S. Churchill' A.
Astilbe 'Federsee' Su.
Dianthus 'Gravetye Gem' Su.
D. 'Old Velvet' Su.
Dicentra 'Bountiful' L.Sp.
Dodecatheon meadia 'Red' Sp.
Helleborus orientalis dark red forms Sp.
Hemerocallis 'Stafford' Su.
Iris 'Cherry Gardens' Su.
Iris sibirica 'Helen Astor' Su.
Lobelia cardinalis H: L.Su.
L. 'Dark Crusader' L.Su.
L. 'Queen Victoria' L.Su.
Lychnis coronaria atrosanguinea Su.
Paeonia 'Dr. H.B. Barnsby' Su.
P. 'Her Majesty' Su.
P. 'King of England' Su.
Penstemon 'Garnet' Su. – A.
P. 'Ruby' Su. – A.
Potentilla astrosanguinea Su.
Primula japonica 'Miller's Crimson' E.Su.
P. 'Valley Red' E.Su.
P. x *wanda* 'Tawny Port' Sp.
Sedum 'Dragon's Blood' L.Su.
Trillium sessile (*T. cunneatum*) Sp.
Viola 'Ruby Queen' Su. – A.

SHRUBS

Chaenomeles 'Crimson and Gold' Sp.
Cytisus 'Burkwoodii' E.Su.
Helianthemum 'Cerise Queen' Su.
H. 'Red Dragon' H:Su.
Hibiscus 'Woodbridge' L.Su. – A.
Magnolia liliflora 'Nigra' L.Sp.
Paeonia suffruticosa 'Duchess of Kent' E.Su.
Rose (cluster-flowered) 'Lilli Marlene' Su.
R. gallica 'Charles de Mills' Su.
R.g. 'Tuscany Superb' Su.
R. rugosa 'Roseraie de l'Haie' E.Su. – A.
R. 'Scarlet Fire' H: Su.

CLIMBERS

Clematis 'Niobe' Su.
Lonicera 'Dropmore Scarlet' H: Su.
Rose 'Allen Chandler' Su.
R. 'Crimson Glory' Su.
R. 'Etoile de Hollande Climbing' Su.
Tropaeoleum speciosum Su.

TREES

Crataegus oxycantha 'Paul's Scarlet' L.Sp.
Embothrium coccineum lanceolatum H: Su.
Malus 'Profusion' L.Sp.

THE YELLOW GARDEN

Yellow is an unfashionable colour in the garden. It has a gaiety which is at variance with the current striving for good taste. As a result, few people plan a golden border, though you have only to see a group of yellow flowers at dusk or a mingling of golden foliage in shade to realize how much they miss. The colour's value to the gardener lies in its ability to shine out and advance to meet the eye. This means that it must be carefully used and it is probably crude handling in the past that gives it its poor image.

At one end of the yellow range come the pale buttery shades: those of the rose 'Mermaid', of primroses, of *Verbascum* 'Gainsborough' and the indispensable *Sisyrinchium striatum*. All these are blenders, good companions for any colour. When partnered with the other side of the spectrum, they are particularly delicate with blue, flattering to violets and at their most ravishing with the purple-crimsons, an infallible association.

The other end of the range includes the egg-yolk yellows and oranges that are partly composed of red. These make their own demands and you can rarely just slip them into an existing border, for they will easily act as thugs, overwhelming

their subtler companions. Better to contrive associations between equals and mix them with scarlets and deep, warm reds to form a hot border.

YELLOW BULBS

Crocus chrysanthus 'Cream Beauty' Sp.
Fritillaria imperialis 'Maxima Lutea' Sp.
Hedychium gardnerianum (T) L.Su. – A.
Iris 'Pogo' L.Sp.
Lilium 'Citronella' Su.
L. 'Limelight' Su.
Narcissus bulbocodium Sp.
N. 'February Gold' Sp.
N. 'Hawera' Sp.
Tulip 'West Point' (lily-flowering) Sp.

PERENNIALS

Asphodeline lutea Su.
Centaurea macrocephala Su.
Cephalaria gigantea Su.
Coreopsis verticillata Su.
Crocosmia 'Solfataire' L.Su.
Digitalis lutea Su.
Euphorbia × *martinii* L.Sp.
E. myrsinites Sp.
E. wulfenii Sp.
Hemerocallis lilio-asphodelus Su.
H. 'Whichford' Su.
Kirengeshoma palmata A.
Kniphofia 'Little Maid' L.Su.
Ligularia stenocephala 'The Rocket' L.Su.
Primula florindae Su.
Rudbeckia 'Herbstsonne' L.Su.
Thalictrum speciosissimum (syn. *T. flavum glaucum*) Su.
Trollius europaeus L.Sp.
Verbascum 'Cotswold Queen' Su.
V. 'Gainsborough' Su.

ANNUALS

Bidens 'Golden Goddess' HHA
Calendula (marigold)
Coreopsis tinctoria
Helianthus annuus (sunflower)
Hibiscus trionum HHA
Hunnemania fumariifolia HHA
Tithonia 'Yellow Torch'

TREES

Koelreuteria paniculata Su.
Laburnum × *watereri* 'Vossii' E.Su.

ABOVE: *Hotly coloured hybrid lilies reinforced by the golden* Spartium junceum *to their rear.*

RIGHT: Lonicera tragophylla, *a scentless honeysuckle that needs shade to thrive.*

Lightness of touch achieved by combining yellow with white.

Seasonal Use

Continuous yellow can be obtrusive to live with and it is best partnered with a succession of different colours throughout the year to give you relief. In spring, it is easy to overplant yellow if you concentrate on the mainstream daffodils. Mix them instead with blue drifts of scillas. In early summer, you might favour yellow and violet: try the tall *Asphodeline lutea* with mounds of *Geranium* × *ibericum*. Later still in the summer, the plant palette can adapt to autumnal shades of, dark red and gold with rudbeckias, heleniums, helianthus and gaillardias. In full autumn, the gold of solidagos may be contrasted by mauve *Aster sedifolius*.

Shape and Colour

The form in which a colour appears in the garden has its own effect which is independent of the shade. A high proportion of the yellow summer flowers belong to the *Compositae* group. Their daisy form has its own engaging simplicity but a border composed predominantly of these flowers can be boring. Their leaves are often dull and you need the liveliness of good foliage plants to import variety and a change of focus.

YELLOW SHRUBS

Fremontodendron
   californicum (T) Su.
Genista aetnensis Su.
Paeonia suffruticosa
   'L'Esperance' E.Su.
Rosa 'Buff Beauty' Su.
R. 'Graham Thomas' Su.
R. rugosa 'Agnes' E.Su.
R. xanthina 'Canary Bird'
   Su.
Rhododendron 'Chikor' Sp.
Rh. luteum L.Sp.
Rh. xanthocodon L.Sp.

CLIMBERS

Clematis orientalis 'Bill
   Mackenzie' L.Su.
C. tangutica L.Su.
Lonicera × *tellmanniana*
   (apricot) Su.
L. tragophylla Su.
Rosa banksiae E.Su.
R. 'Climbing Lady
   Hillingdon' Su.
R. 'Easlea's Golden
   Rambler' Su.
R. 'Mermaid' Su.
R. 'Reve d'Or' Su.

GOLDEN FOLIAGE: PERENNIALS

Filipendula ulmaria 'Aurea' F
Hakonechloa macra 'Albo-aurea'
Hosta 'Gold Standard'
H. 'Sunburst'
Millium effusum 'Aureum' F
Sagina glabra 'Aurea' (carpeter)

SHRUBS

Acer japonicum 'Aureum'
Choisya ternata 'Sundance'
Juniperus 'Pfitzerana Aurea' F
Lonicera 'Baggeson's Gold' F
Sambucus racemosa 'Plumosa Aurea'
Taxus baccata 'Repens Aurea' F

CLIMBERS

Hedera helix 'Buttercup' F
Humulus lupulus 'Aureus' F

TREES

Catalpa bignonioides 'Aurea'
Gleditsia triacanthos 'Sunburst' F
Robinia pseudoacacia 'Frisia'

Gold and green with Caragana arborescens, junipers, acer and hostas.

Golden Foliage

This has its own light, creating the illusion of sunshine in even a gloomy corner. Yet this is often the position to trigger the instability that is inherent in some gold leaves which habitually revert to green in heavy shade. Others, perversely, will scorch in sunlight. And there are those, regardless of position which will make a bright spring start but fade greenly as the weeks pass. No reason to avoid them, but bear in mind your effects will be in a state of flux – more interesting than have them frozen in stasis. (Those that tend to fade for whatever reason are marked F in the following plant lists.)

Of the three groups, the most awkward are those that refuse to remain gold in deep shade, which is their *raison d'être* for a gardener. Try instead to give these a dark background whether deep green ivy or conifers.

More rarely, golden-leafed plants can present you with a problem peculiarly theirs when their flowers clash with their leaves. Certain spiraeas and *Fuchsia* 'Genii' with their yellow leaves and bright rose flowers are garish for this reason alone.

Strong shapes and textures contribute to a successful green garden; the grass Stipa gigantea backed by Ozothamnus rosmarinifolius, Crambe cordifolia and the silver Hippophae rhamnoides.

THE GREEN GARDEN

G reen is usually treated as wallpaper in a colour garden, because of its background role. Yet green is a colour in its own right when it is thoughtfully deployed as a star rather than downgraded into a foil. Its virtue when used on its own lies in its restfulness, soothing to the eye on a hot day in summer, yet substantial enough to quicken the winter garden to life if it is evergreen.

GRASSES

Deschampsia caespitosa 'Gold Veil': panicles in summer;
    3 × 3ft/90 × 90cm.
Miscanthus sinensis 'Silver Feather': silky pale plumes in
    autumn; 7 × 7ft/2.1 × 2.1m.
M. s. 'Zebrinus': cross-banded gold; fawn plumes in autumn;
    5 × 5ft/1.5 × 1.5m.
Stipa calamagrostis: feathery flowers in summer;
    3 – 4 × 2ft/1 – 1.2m × 60cm.
S. gigantea: glorious oaten flowers in summer;
    6 × 3ft/1.8 × 1m. E

BAMBOOS

Arundinaria murielae: bright green, clump-forming;
    6 – 9ft/2 – 3m. E
Phyllostachys nigra 'Boryana': clump-forming; arching
    stems; 9 – 12ft/2.5 – 4m. E
Sinarundinaria nitida: slender canes, narrow-leafed;
    8 – 12ft/2.2 – 4m. E

LEFT: A highly formal layout with mostly evergreen structure.

Knowing Your Ferns

An intimate acquaintance with ferns is the first essential when making a green garden in semi-shade. Though many are lumbered with portmanteau names, it is worth putting faces to them as their range and delicacy of leaf are a joy to the gardener who grows them. You can use the tall, vase-like ferns as backgrounds or as central pivots around which you place the more tabulate ferns. Or use rhythmically the vertical and horizontal ferns, remembering not to over-crowd the latter or their shape will be lost.

Designing a Green Garden

The good green garden depends more than other colour gardens on its structure, for whilst there are shades of green, there is insufficient contrast between these tints for them to be used as structural colour blocks. Variety of emphatic leaf shape and firm garden design are essential.

The key to designing this sort of colour garden is to imagine either that you are colour-blind or that you are viewing your scheme in a black and white photograph. If your design and proposed blend of plants hold your interest despite being subjected to these constraints, then your plan will be successful.

Start with a firm structure of evergreens, perhaps a low box hedge or a pattern of clipped conifers or the small-leafed evergreen hebes like H. 'Edinensis'. Their stiffness can form the unbending framework for plants of more fluid habit like grasses, which can spray out within their confines. One of the special assets of grasses are their tall flowering plumes in summer which mean they have more to offer than just foliage plants.

Green foliage has, however, its own kind of potential. It varies not only in its shape but in its light-reflecting qualities. Yew for example is dense, velvety and light-absorbent, whereas the bold leaves of Fatsia japonica or the winter-berrying Iris foetidissima are shiny. Both extremes have their place.

Green flowers add seasonal change, vital to avoid monotony in a green garden. Choose them for contrast, from the lime-green froth of Alchemilla mollis to the sculptured spathes of Zantedeschia 'Green Goddess'. The euphorbias are essential for their distinguished habit of growth and frog-spawn flowers. Add pots of greenish lilies like 'Limelight' or the enchanting half-hardy annual Nicotiana langsdorfii with its tubular green bells.

FERNS

Adiantum pedatum: dark fronds like a bird's foot; 2 × 2ft/60 × 60cm.

Athyrium filix-femina plumosum: lacy, light green, spreading; 2 × 2ft/60 × 60cm.

Dryopteris filix-mas cristata: robust with crests on pinnae and apex of fronds; 3 × 2ft/90 × 60cm.

Matteuccia struthiopteris: light green with short trunk; almost rampant spreader in moist soils, 3 – 5ft high/1 – 1.5m.

Polystichum setiferum plumosum divisilobum: elite light green fern with laciest fronds, horizontal; 2 × 2ft/60 × 60cm.

GREEN FLOWERS

Angelica archangelica
(biennial)
Eryngium agavifolium
(perennial)
Euphorbia × *martinii* (sub-
shrubby perennial) E
E. characias ssp. wulfenii
(s.s. perennial) E
E. robbiae (s.s. per.) can be
rampant E
Galtonia viridiflora (bulb)
Helleborus foetidus
(perennial) E
Moluccella laevis HHA
Nicotiana langsdorfii HHA
Zantedeschia 'Green
Goddess' (perennial)
Zigadenus elegans
(perennial)

Grasses including miscanthus, pennisetum, stipa; also ferns
(polystichum).

Variegated Foliage

One can add variety to the green garden by including variegated foliage, but some of the brighter combinations are going to shatter the peacefulness. This is less true of green and cream than gold and green, and the latter may find a more comfortable home in the gold-foliaged border (see page 41). But even cream and green leaves are most suitably kept to a very small proportion of the whole, used to lighten the darkest greens or dropped into a gloomy corner. These plants all suffer from a lack of chlorophyll and tend to grow more slowly than their green equivalents. Some also revert when your back is turned, usually those that carry their blotch of non-green on the centre of their leaves rather than at the margins.

GOLD AND GREEN FOLIAGE

Acorus gramineus 'Ogon' (grass)
Arundinara (Pleioblastus) viridistrata (bamboo)
Hosta fortunei 'Aureomarginata' (perennial)
Ilex 'Golden King' (female holly)
Iris pallida 'Aurea Variegata' (perennial)
I. pseudacorus bastardii (perennial)
Salvia officinalis 'Icterina' (shrub)
Symphytum grandiflorum 'Variegatum' (perennial)

CLIMBERS

Hedera helix 'Goldheart'
H.h. 'Marmorata Minor'

GREEN AND CREAM FOLIAGE

Aralia elata 'Variegata' (shrub)
Astrantia major 'Sunningdale' (perennial)
Cornus alba 'Elegantissima' (shrub)
C. controversa 'Variegata' (shrub)
Cotoneaster horizontalis 'Variegata' (shrub)
Eryngium variifolium (perennial)
Ilex aquifolium 'Handsworth New Silver' (female holly)
Symphoricarpos orbiculatus 'Foliis Variegatis' (shrub)

CLIMBERS

Hedera helix 'Clotted Cream'
H.h. 'Glacier'

Carmine peonies are the brighter against dark yews, lead-green cistus, glaucous santolina, blue-green rue and silver Stachys byzantina.

Silver and Grey Foliage

G rey is too indeterminate a colour to merit its own quarters and a uniformly silver garden would lack the positive qualities of its green equivalent. This has nothing to do with the merits of the plants which sport this colour leaf and these include some of the most aristocratic one can grow. For this reason a green and grey foliage garden can be a highly desirable creation – restful yet full of light and texture, especially if you position the darker blocks against their lighter neighbours, exploiting the principle of brightness contrast.

Use silver in the white garden (pages 18 – 21) and the crimson garden (page 35), and wherever you need a barrier between potentially violent clashes. Use it too in the autumn garden (page 58) where it is a smoky background to the reds.

SILVER FOLIAGE

Artemisia 'Powis Castle' (low shrub)
A. schmidtiana 'Nana'.
Hebe 'Quicksilver' (shrub)
H. 'Pewter Dome'
Helichrysum angustifolium (shrub)
Ozothamnus rosmarinifolius 'Silver Jubilee' (shrub)
Pyrus salicifolia 'Pendula' (tree)
Salvia argentea (biennial/perennial)
Stachys byzantina 'Cotton Boll' (perennial)

PURPLE FOLIAGE (see also 'The Purple Garden', page 26, and 'The Red Garden', page 35)

Cimicifuga ramosa 'Brunette' (perennial)
Cotinus coggygria 'Foliis Purpureis' (shrub)
Dahlia 'Bishop of Llandaff' (HHBulb)
Sambucus 'Guincho Purple' (shrub)
Vitis vinifera 'Purpurea' (cl.)

COLOR COMBINATIONS

Paeonia tenuifolia *and the lily-flowering tulip 'Captain Fryatt':* *the red and the green have a mutually brightening effect.*

In the previous section, I have suggested combinations which will flatter predominant hues. These harmonies exemplify Chevreul's theories (pages 10–11). However, gardens are three-dimensional and colours in the distance, beyond the selected combinations, are quite likely to be caught by the eye. In this case, you have to bear in mind the phenomenon of simultaneous contrast. You also need to consider it when you are making a border of mixed colours.

Colour Injury

The point at which a colour injures rather than merely affects its neighbour is somewhat subjective for we are not passive recorders of colour phenomena. Not only our eyes but our brains interpret them in terms of our own experience and expectations. However, most people who are sensitive to the effect of colour would agree that injury does take place. Usually the degree of harm depends on the proportions of one colour to another and on whether each is a fully saturated colour or whether one or both are tints (pale versions – the colour with an admixture of white) or shades (deep versions – the colour with an admixture of black). Tints and shades will almost always soften effects.

Simultaneous Contrast

When you see two juxtaposed colours, they will appear as dissimilar as possible as shown in the table below.

Effect on left-hand colour	Juxtaposed colours	Effect on right-hand colour
more orange	YELLOW/GREEN	more blue
more orange	YELLOW/BLUE	more indigo
more yellow	GREEN/BLUE	more indigo
more purple	VIOLET/BLUE	more green
more yellow	ORANGE/VIOLET	more blue
more violet	RED/ORANGE	more yellow
more orange	RED/BLUE	more green
more green	YELLOW/ORANGE	more red
more orange-red	RED/VIOLET	more blue
more green	YELLOW/RED	more purple
more yellow	GREEN/VIOLET	more purple
more blue	GREEN/ORANGE	more red
brighter	YELLOW/VIOLET	brighter
brighter	ORANGE/BLUE	brighter
brighter	RED/GREEN	brighter

What is happening is that each colour adopts the tinge of the complementary of its neighbour. A gardener who wants to plant blocks of flowers which have pure colours (rare in Nature) needs to bear this in mind. It must be said that this approach to colour-planting has been much abused with carpet-bedding (e.g. scarlet salvias and blue lobelias planted in equal quantities). However, it can be successful if the harmonies are preserved and if the blocks of colour are of unequal size – as they should be (see page 16); but you need to remember that the smaller area will always be the more affected by simultaneous contrast.

Fatal Injury

My own interpretation of injury is that point at which colours, when juxtaposed, rob each other of their potential beauty, delicacy or richness. This is not to say that they are ugly together, but there is a falling-off in the quality of each. The eye cannot focus satisfactorily on a combination of shell-pink and bright red, for example. They are incompatible – though, since one of the colours is a tint, the effect is not so violent as when two incompatible hues are partnered.

Nor will the eye tolerate the disruption of an isolated different colour in a tonal border of related hues e.g. just one yellow plant in a long border of soft blues transferring to lavender. The yellow plant will act as a rootless delinquent. Yet plan to incorporate buttery yellows or soft apricots in small drifts related to the cool shades around, and they would appear as harmonious patches of light in shadows. They would advance and the blues and lavenders recede, creating depth in the border.

Proportion and balance will alter the aesthetic effect almost as much as the colours themselves.

ABOVE: *The purple-red rose 'Zigeunerknabe', flattered by both the creamy* Digitalis lutea *and the pink rose 'De Meaux' is the key to this wonderful colour mix.*

Breaking the Rules

Nature, however, is not polite and obedient and a reminder is in order that she breaks rules herself, sometimes with the liveliest effects. It is possible for us to plan too safely. I recall a vignette in early winter of deep orange pyracantha berries beside pink nerines. It was a cheering shout of defiance before colourless winter took over.

GRAVEL GARDENS AND 'ALPINE' GARDENS

G ravel gardens are hot, for they are usually made in open areas of the garden where their stone reflects the sun. This in turn affects the plants. These grow swiftly, having warm heads and moist feet, as their roots spread beneath the gravel mulch. The result is that a gravel garden is likely to have a lush cover of leaf and flower. Add to this the preference of plants to sow themselves in the gravel, and you have all the ingredients for the most high-powered and high density part of the garden.

Such a place can take colour at its most brilliant and should be exploited to do so. Its residents can be confidently drawn from the warm parts of the world, for they stand a chance of surviving in a gravel garden even in cooler climates. The heat reflected from the particles of stone ripens the wood of the plants and makes them more resistant to the scourges of winter. It is the place where even the more tender Mediterranean cistus or the South African osteospermums may prove reliably permanent.

The Need for Colour

T he case for brilliant colour depends on more than its mere appropriateness in the gravel garden. It is actually necessary, because gravel – whether fawn, grey or rufous – has a bleaching effect in high sunshine on the more softly coloured flowers. Unlike green lawns which set off other colours, it affords no colour contrast to throw the blossoms into relief. Instead it reflects the light and the flowers are dimmed by being bleached not only by light overhead but from the ground. Caught in this pincer effect, only an intense and glowing colour scheme will survive.

Choosing Colours

Flowers alone will not give the colour effects you seek. Foliage, too, is essential – for without green (and its bluish and greyish variants), a colour we unwisely take for granted, the flower colours will lack a binding background.

The very heat of a gravel garden on a blazing day dictates the omission of certain colours. Scarlets, yellows and oranges will make it seem oppressive and the garden will become a place to be glimpsed briefly and not lingered in. For this reason, better to keep to the cooler side of the spectrum – which does not imply reducing the brilliance of colour. The strong hot pinks of *Cistus x purpureus*, violet carpeters like *Hebe* 'Carl Teschner', the rubies of *Penstemon* 'Garnet' or the purple-reds of *Rosa rugosa* 'Roseraie de l'Haie' are desirable here. So too are the intense blues of agapanthus, whose globular heads and prolific flowering make them a focus of attention. Whites will act as spotlights – whether the milky gleam of cistus or the creamier shades of yuccas or the pure true white of *Libertia grandiflora*, or the foam of *Crambe cordifolia*.

To these one can add foliage plants in a range of greens: perhaps the dark *Ozothamnus rosmarinifolius* or the green tufts of the grass *Stipa gigantea* or the blue grass *Helictotrichon sempervirens*. These are plant pictures for high summer, strongly yet not hotly coloured.

ABOVE: *Wide spectrum of colour in this gravel garden, but links are made between the blues of flowers and foliage; the sulphur of the rose 'Mermaid' and Sisyrinchium striatum; and the purple reds of the rugosa rose 'Roseraie de l'Haie' and the violet Clematis 'Etoile Violette'.*

'Alpine' Gardens

Although traditionally the dwarf plants of the alpine garden differ from those of the hot Mediterranean gravel garden, it sometimes shares a common medium in having a stone-covered surface that is used to simulate scree. To this extent, it shares the same obstacles to the successful use of colour. These obstacles can be overcome in the same way, though greater emphasis needs to be placed on foliage carpeting plants to provide the green. Thymes in variety, green acaena, azorella, and sedums are helpful, so are the ground-hugging junipers.

There is a colour problem, however, that is particularly challenging with alpines or rock plants: namely, to contrive flowers for later in the year. There is a big spring and summer burst but little afterwards unless one plans. To secure a late-season performance, it pays to include a selection of the following plants: gentians (*G. sino-ornata* and *G. septemfida* are among the easier), blue, pink and white *Platycodon grandiflorus*, *Sedum* 'Ruby Glow' and *S.* 'Dragon's Blood', the white, violet or blue forms of *Viola cornuta*, white *Nierembergia rivularis*, *Sempervivella alba*, and the violet *Origanum laevigatum*, to which pink diascias in variety can be added for a non-stop show. No polygonums (now called *Persicaria*)? They certainly add late colour, but a show of colour cannot turn a plant into a first-rate act.

49

RIGHT: Iris pseudacorus, *a large iris for wet areas which will self-seed, so it is best kept for big ponds.*

THE WATER GARDEN

The wise gardener uses colour warily in the water garden, for it holds a mirror up to his mistakes. Errors of judgement come in double doses: once on the ground and, again, in their reflection. This is not the only reason to respect the reflective quality of water. Some ponds can mirror adjacent buildings, trees and blue sky, all of which can be every bit as dominant in the mirror as they are in reality.

Water-gardening is practised in three different forms: on the surface of the pool (with water-lilies); around the periphery (with aquatic marginals); and in the adjacent bog-garden which is a reliably moist version of a border and often shares the same plants. Water-gardening can also be formal or informal, either of which may have a restraining effect on the application of colour. Formal gardens look better clothed in more organized arrangements of colour whereas the informal may be dressed in more relaxed groupings.

Surface Colour

Water-lilies are the most widely grown of the hardy deep water aquatics. With the exception of blue, they produce flowers in the full range of colour through white, vinous-red, and pink on the cool side of the spectrum to yellow and orange-red on the hot side. On a small pond (and even on a large one, unless it lends itself to segregated areas) it would be unwise to mix warm with cool which would flout the tranquility of the scene. In areas with long hot summers, there is an argument for favouring the cool side only: it gives you the licence to add the ravishing blue-lilac half-hardy aquatic called *Eichhornia crassipes*.

How you deploy the water lilies will also have an effect on the colour. The lilies should cover only a portion of the water, which means colour will be confined to a particular area, making a pattern in itself, composed of the dark reflective pond on the one hand and the sporadic sparks of colour on the other. Secondly, those sparks of colour will become increasingly frugal if you are growing the lilies in a basket, unless you lift and divide them every few years. Congestion will otherwise lead to diminishing leaf-size and reduced flowering.

Recommended varieties for up to 3ft/90cm of water:
◇ *Nymphaea* 'Marliacea Albida', pure white, fragrant.
◇ *N.* 'James Brydon', deep rose, dark purplish-green leaves.
◇ *N.* 'Rose Arey', pink ageing to crimson.
◇ *N.* 'Marliacea Chromatella', rich yellow.
◇ *N.* 'Graziella', orange-red (for up to 2ft/60cm of water).

Marginal Aquatics

These grow in wet mud or shallow water around the edge of the pool and are therefore the most likely to be reflected in the water. Irises make the main show and are of such refined and statuesque beauty that they merit a sympathetic colour scheme during their summer flowering. The blue *Pontederia cordata* with bold spires of blossoms in late summer could maintain the cool theme dictated by the water-lilies and two out of the three irises listed below:

◊ *Iris laevigata* The type is sky-blue but innumerable cultivars range from pink to icy white to violet and white. 3 ft/90 cm.

◊ *I. pseudacorus* Only for the large or natural pond. A prolific display of yellow flowers in early summer. The form 'Bastardii' has primrose and white leaves in spring and early summer and is more compact. Can look gaudy unless carefully placed. 4 ft/1.2m.

◊ *I. versicolor* Violet-purple North American native; the form 'Kermesina' has exquisite plum-purple blooms. 2½ ft/75 cm.

Bog Plants

The challenge here is to put the foot on the brake and aim for coherence. Primula varieties in particular come in so many clashing shades like bright yellow and shocking pink that it is easy to have a distressing riot around the pool and pretend it is cheerful. Those who like both colours can eat their cake and keep it by ensuring that the clashing plants don't bloom simultaneously. This way you might include, say, *Primula japonica* 'Miller's Crimson' and *P. pulverulenta* with magenta blossoms for early summer, and the tall *P. helodoxa* with golden flowers to follow in late summer. Where you do find yourself with colour clashes, the cool green leaves of hostas or ferns like *Matteuccia struthiopteris* or *Onoclea sensibilis* are particularly helpful in toning down the temperature.

Mimulus are another riot-prone species in yellow, scarlet, pink and spotty combinations. Again, they need a firm hand to ensure the best effects, especially since they flower for a long time and can harmonize with a companion plant whilst clashing with its successor a month later.

Bright bog primulas are cooled by green foliage.

RIGHT: *A colour-related grouping of pots includes verbenas, pelargoniums and the dark-foliaged succulent* Aeonium arboreum atropurpureum.

COLOR SCHEMES FOR POTS

Pots and tubs are one of the ornamental accessories of the garden. Like hats or handbags, they are secondary to the main clothes but make an impression in their own right. Their job is therefore demanding and sometimes contradictory: this confection of the garden must not only look glamorous yet sympathize with its environment.

To this end, it helps to keep them simple yet plan them with an eye on their surroundings. A very large pot on an unplanted terrace might take a maximum of four plants in a blend of colour. Its bravura display will be interesting and jazzy enough for it to take on the role of star entertainer. But in surroundings which are already fussed with plants, there is a better argument for planting a single specimen in a pot – one colour presented in a clear shape which will provide the onlooker with a focus.

Colour Constraints

The colour schemes you adopt must depend on the surroundings, and the same constraints on the use of colour apply to plants, whether potted or in open ground. When you use colour in a pot, positioning it against a planted background, you are in effect combining the pot plants with others in the open ground. The simpler the ingredients, the clearer the statement. One most beautiful example is the white *Lilium* 'Olivia' presented in a stone pot on a plinth, in front of a clipped yew hedge.

Indeed white against a dark green background can scarcely be improved. It is pure, confident and emphatic – in other words, the perfect choice for a starring role. You would achieve a more relaxed effect with a white geranium like the glistening, purple-marked *Pelargonium* 'White Unique'. Though less statuesque and film-starry than lilies, it would give you spread rather than height and be slightly more tolerant of neglect. It also has the advantage of blooming from early summer until late autumn or frosts.

There is an additional constraint that is peculiar to pot gardening, for it is imposed by the colour of pot. This is not always a flattering accompaniment to its plant. Neutral stone or mossy concrete will be as unobtrusive as one could wish. But a red geranium in a terracotta pot can take on the colour of a furious tomato – in some surroundings perhaps ideal, at one extreme, but in others very probably disastrous.

Non-stop Colour

Since pots are usually planted with a view to non-stop bloom for four months, this imposes another colour constraint. Their shades must harmonize with the successional bloom of the garden around them, even though the latter's colour schemes may change. If, however, an unforeseen clash attacks you, the problem is easily resolved by the portable nature of, at least, the lighter-weight pots. You can re-position them in more congenial surroundings elsewhere in the garden.

Grouping the Display

You can also group pots together to make colour associations amongst themselves. A pot of pink fuchsia can be flanked with containers of the purple heliotrope; or in a shadier corner, pots of hostas and ferns could be assembled. In late spring, containers of silver and green variegated ivy like *Hedera helix* 'Glacier' could be gathered around the white bleeding heart, *Dicentra spectabilis* 'Alba'.

This is not simply an artistic ploy. It works in your favour too in that it takes the onerousness out of maintaining pots. They are the most demanding form of gardening, always asking for water, never satisfied. By making a small assembly, you can douse them all together.

Good Combinations

◊ *Fuchsia* 'Display' with pink corolla and lilac sepals, combined with a trailing blue lobelia or with the white, mauve-spotted annual *Nemophila maculata*.

◊ Violet petunias and trailing variegated ivy; or maroon petunias and *Helichrysum* 'Limelight'.

◊ The trailing blue *Convolvulus sabatius* (syn. *C. mauritanicus*) around the apricot *Mimulus glutinosus*.

◊ The trailing, dark-red, ivy-leafed *Pelargonium* 'Mexican Beauty' with purple heliotrope ('Chatsworth' is one of the best scented forms).

◊ The pink *Argyranthemum* 'Vancouver' with the grey-leafed *Helichrysum petiolare*.

COLOR IN THE WILD OR WOODLAND GARDEN

The keynote in these areas of the garden is restraint, for one has to efface one's own palette in favour of another approach. The cue must come from Nature in any part of the garden that is or affects to be natural. This does not mean that the gardener's impositions are artless – colour-cunning is as necessary here as in the formal garden – but it does mean the art must be concealed by an impression of naturalness.

In the natural wilderness or woodland, it is usual for a process of colonization to take place by the dominant plant of the season. In spring, it might be primroses and pale anemones, white wild garlic and bluebells. In summer, possibly the purplish-red betony in open ground, followed by the little blue scabious in later summer. In each case there is a carpet of the main flower, and, though others blossom, they do so in lesser numbers.

Colour Effects in Nature

The effect this has on colour is to simplify it. Either a single colour predominates, or where several flowers thrive with equal vigour, a combination prevails: perhaps violets and cowslips in woodland or, in open ground at a later stage of the year, the intensely violet-blue *Geranium pratense* and the milky white meadowsweet, *Filipendula ulmaria*. This limited colour palette produces astonishing harmonies and effects of great richness. It also gives the wilderness an artistic unity that the gardener changes at his peril.

Camassia esculenta naturalized in grass.

How to Contrive Natural Effects

The problem for most gardeners is not whether they want to imitate nature – most do – but how to. With bulbs, there is no difficulty. It is simple to buy bulk loads of individual wild species and scatter them in innocent-looking drifts across the ground for naturalizing. The lavender *Crocus tommasinianus*, snowdrops, wild daffodils (*Narcissus pseudo-narcissus*), the blue *Anemone apennina, Chionodoxa luciliae*, the duskily chequered snakes-head fritillary all lend themselves to this treatment. If you avoid mixing them, and avoid discordant introductions, they will quickly effect the simplicity you are trying to convey.

However, the gardener is not so easily served with herbaceous plants as bulbs. Seedsmen often provide these in mixtures which will look spotty and confused on the ground. A sensible solution, though not without nuisance, is to buy the seed of individual species of your choice and establish these as you would for a herbaceous border – by raising seedlings in a separate plot, growing them on and planting them out in wandering drifts and large patches in areas clear of turf. This has two advantages. Firstly, the plants are stronger, will establish themselves more vigorously and, if you scatter friable earth around them, will seed themselves into colonies, thus reinforcing the effect you are seeking. Secondly, you can control the density and mix of the colours you introduce.

ABOVE LEFT: *Colour-related rhododendrons.*

ABOVE RIGHT: Camellia *'Leonard Messel' backed by the paler Magnolia × loebneri 'Leonard Messel'.*

Planting Woodland Shrubs

Once again, the most beautiful effects are achieved by the simplest use of colour. Camellias and magnolias in white and pink enchant, but multi-coloured jamborees of azaleas appal. Woodland is no place for a carnival, though this does not mean that strong hues like rubies or violets are out of place. Rather their single notes will glow the more intensely in the green shade – but only as long as they are controlled and not assailed by a mix of other colours.

Malus 'Lemoinei' underplanted with Smilacena racemosa.

THE SPRING GARDEN

It is in spring that colour can seem at its most raw. In the northern hemisphere, it erupts suddenly after its winter absence. Here, too, it is usually seen against a leafless background in which green, the normal unifier and blender, is absent. Unless plants are naturalized in grass, the background colour for their blooms is therefore the dark brown of earth, not a canvas anyone would prefer.

One solution is to plant bulbs around and amongst evergreen and evergrey shrubs, or with plants that produce foliage early in the year. There are not too many examples of the latter category but Gertrude Jekyll recommended using both *Myrrhis odorata* and *Veratrum nigrum* which produce elegant yet contrasting early foliage. She also included *Euphorbia wulfenii* and a good addition nowadays would be hemerocallis whose pale green tufts of leaves start to thrust through in the earliest spring.

Dominant Yellow

An earthy background is one difficulty in the spring. Another problem is posed by the predominance of yellow. Daffodils have such a stranglehold on the spring garden that yellow is the only colour associated with spring. Sad, because egg-yolk yellow – the colour of the most common daffodils – is an excluder, ill-becoming to pink especially.

Perverse though it may seem, there is a sound artistic case for planting only white daffodils and narcissi, for these open the garden to the full range of spring colour – violets, pinks, blues, creams, a spectrum that is consistently fresh and harmonious, and which can accommodate the burgundies of some magnolias or the blue-reds of selected camellias without seeming crude.

Placing Colour

The temptation, and if followed it is a mistake, is to plant one colour in overlarge blocks in the spring garden. It is easily enough done because we are so reliant on bulbs for the main impact and these rarely make a show if planted in smaller groups. Maintenance, too, demands central grouping when plants are naturalized in grass. Since their leaves cannot be cut down until they have started to die naturally, it is easier to mow round a single block than a number.

A carpet of plum, green and ivory hellebores.

Colour from Bulbs

One way to enliven a scheme is to infiltrate tiny brush strokes of different colours within the block. It might be a single occasional red tulip amongst a drift of white daffodils or a peppering of blue scillas amongst a sea of soft yellow jonquils. These act as a spice, relieving the blandness.

There is less scope for placing colour in a border, but only because bulbs, the most obvious source of spring colour, are rarely planned inmates of a mixed border but are added at a later stage after the key plants are established. Bulbs in a border are therefore usually gap-fillers, a role which diminishes them. Even so, they can be infiltrated more advantageously than is usually the case. One of the best examples can be seen at Sissinghurst where clusters of the small blue *Ipheion uniflorum* 'Wisley Blue' are planted beside peonies. Summer-flowering peonies present a large gap in the spring border for they are late to produce their shoots, yet have an eventual spread of 3 – 4ft/1 – 1.2m. They therefore provide plenty of space for small bulbs – and in this case a good colour combination too, for their shoots are dark red and the ipheions' blossoms a soft blue.

Dying leaves

Even the loveliest colour scheme can be spoilt by an intractable difficulty with bulbs whose dying leaves can ruin a border just when it is pumping up to its grand horticultural performance. The yellow-brown of decay is not a colour to encourage. Herbaceous plants whose foliage provides a canopy after the bulbs have flowered (such as the peonies just mentioned) will hide the dying leaves. Otherwise, late-flowering varieties of bulbs which you have planted in front of the earlier flowering bulbs will help them decay discreetly.

Suggested Colour Combinations

◊ White snowdrops and *Lamium maculatum* 'Beacon Silver'.
◊ *Tulipa* 'White Emperor' and the blue grass *Helictotrichon sempervirens* and the silvery carpeter, *Artemisia schmidtiana* 'Nana'.

◊ White *Narcissus* 'Thalia', pink bergenias and blue rue.
◊ Yellow *Narcissus* 'Hawera' and lavender-blue *Phlox subulata* 'Emerald Cushion'.
◊ Blue *Scilla sibirica* 'Spring Beauty' and Bowles' Golden Grass (*Milium effusum* 'Aureum').

THE AUTUMN GARDEN

Colour in the autumn garden is challenging to manage for it is transitional. At this period you are presented with the problem of juggling the prolonged flowerers of late summer against a backcloth of leaves which is initially green but is now beginning to yellow or turn scarlet. Harmonies can be threatened for in practice one may be faced with flowers from the cool side of the spectrum (mauve asters, purple or pink penstemons) which are displayed against flaming leaves from the hot spectrum. This may look thrilling, but can equally turn out garish. This is one reason why people with spacious gardens often set aside an area to establish plants with the most brilliantly colouring leaves.

Where this is impracticable, the best plan is to try and place your key autumn foliage plants beside amenable companions. This might mean planting a scarlet acer against dark conifers, or the climber, *Parthenocissus henryana*, with white veined ruby leaves in autumn, on a wall near silvery shrubs like *Salix lanata*. In each case you make your point more effectively than if you plant your autumn colouring in squadrons.

Autumn fruit

The same holds true of the berrying shrubs which are every bit as showy as those with coloured foliage. They are also just as necessary for they give a different feeling to the garden – leaves, however gorgeous, are the expression of fading, whereas fruit is the climax of ripeness. Most, however, are harvested by the birds, so it is best to choose the more durable kinds listed opposite if colour is not to fly out of the garden.

Berries can be just as demanding to place as autumn-colouring foliage. Rose-hips in particular may present you with colour clashes. These will steal up on you if you place, for example, rugosa roses which produce tomato-like hips against bluish-pink repeat-flowering roses which are in their second autumnal flush.

The above may sound over-fastidious but one point about autumn colour is its brevity in some areas. In colder regions, it can last for only a fortnight before blustery rain blows the leaves away – all the more important for the colour-conscious gardener to welcome its presence rather than regret it for the way it disrupts his colour harmonies.

RIGHT: *The large hips of* Rosa rugosa *are as brilliantly showy as flowers.*

SHRUBS FOR AUTUMN FOLIAGE

Acer japonicum
   'Aconitifolium'
A.j. 'Vitifolium'
A. palmatum 'Heptalobum
   Osakazuki'
Cotinus coggygria
Fothergilla major

SHRUBS FOR AUTUMN FRUIT (red unless otherwise stated)

Clerodendrum trichotomum
   fargesii (blue berries held
   in a ruby star-shaped
   calyx)
Cotoneaster lacteus
Euonymus cornutus
   quinquecornutus
E. europaeus 'Red Cascade'
E. yedoensis (pink berries)
Rosa moyesii 'Geranium'
R. rugosa 'Alba'
Viburnum opulus
   'Compactum'
V.o. 'Notcutts Variety'
V.o. 'Fructoluteo' (yellow
   berries)

CLIMBERS

Parthenocissus henryana
Vitis coignetiae
V. vinifera 'Brandt'

TREES FOR AUTUMN FOLIAGE (unless otherwise stated)

Arbutus unedo E (for
   'strawberry' fruits)
Cercidiphyllum japonicum
Crataegus × prunifolia
Liquidambar styraciflua (see
   text)
Sorbus sargentiana

Choosing varieties

*A*cers are one of the starting-points but they should carry a buyer-beware label, for the name of the acer does not necessarily guarantee a good form. Seedlings will vary greatly; a yellow acer, for example, is often the progeny of a red-leafed form. One needs to be sure that the acer has been propagated vegetatively from a good form, or take the precaution of buying it only in autumn when the colour has developed in the infant plant.

The same buyer-beware label should hang on a larger tree, *Liquidambar styraciflua*, for again seedlings vary in autumn colour. If you cannot choose it at the time it performs, it would be wiser to buy the clone 'Worplesdon' or 'Lane Roberts', which is as dark as port wine, from a reputable nursery.

Crocus laevigatus fontenayi *is a true winter-flowering crocus.*

THE WINTER GARDEN

The thought of the winter garden does not usually inspire polychromatic visions in the mind. Green is usually both first base and last stop for people, often in its dingiest form like *Viburnum tinus* and the more ubiquitous conifers. But whilst the green (or, rather, evergreen) garden is the most obvious form of the winter garden, it can be transformed into a desirable creation if it is planned with the same degree of care as 'The Green Garden' (see page 42).

The Evergreen Rule

The rule with evergreens is to use them with purpose. They are emphatically not the bits of the garden left over after the star-studded bulk of plants has gone into hibernation. Instead, they are the first bones of the garden, its order and its structure, destined to star in their own right when the summer clutter has died down. And if spread round the garden, pushed into its furthest corners and used as a conscious attempt to furnish throughout, they will make the garden seem clothed all the year.

An even livelier pattern can be crafted if they are knitted in with evergreys which will bring light to their shade (see page 43).

Winter Flowers

It is against this background that one thinks of other colours. Most are occasional luxuries in all but the dedicated winter garden, for, in a seasonally mixed area, one would not want winter-flowering plants to monopolize an area that is more appropriately used for summer-flowerers.

Many shrubs blossom in winter, so does the odd tree, the odd climber, and a number of perennials and bulbs, but in every case each should be judged by more than the flowers or the colour they supply. Is it a good plant as a whole? This is the criterion for its inclusion, for each must be assessed for its leaf and habit as well. Otherwise the search for colour at any price will lead to a garden clothed with plants that are dull for most of the year. Anyone can devise a colour-packed garden for winter with pink and mauve heathers and golden conifers, but it will simply look garish in its season and unimaginative stodge for the rest of the year.

Winter Shrubs

Daphne odora 'Aureo-marginata' E
Fatsia japonica E
Garrya elliptica 'James Roof' E
Hamamelis mollis
Mahonia lomariifolia E
M. 'Charity' E
Rhododendron mucronulatum

Climbers

Clematis balearica, pale green
Jasminum nudiflorum, yellow

Daphne mezereum *against a patterned birch trunk.*

Positioning Winter Colour

The best plants merit the gentlest treatment at this inhospitable time of the year. Although many stand up to fairly harsh weather, their blossoms can still be shredded or browned by scourging wind and it is wiser to give them a sheltered position, such as the lee of the house – nice for them, nice too for the fair-weather gardener, peering from the window without stirring forth himself.

For some white or pastel flowers, even shelter is insufficient. They have to be shielded as well from morning sun, which will damage them in frost. This is especially true of the early-flowering double white camellias which will brown at once.

Winter Bark

This at least is unaffected by the harshest winter weather and trees with patterned trunks will supply columns of quiet colour, perhaps at their most impressive in snow. But, again, the same tough criteria apply for including winter bark in the garden. Are the plants worthy of space for the rest of the year?

BULBS

Crocus ancyrensis, yellow
C. imperatii, violet within, fawn with brown stripes outside
C. laevigatus fontenayi, pale violet-blue
Cyclamen coum, crimson-purple
Iris danfordiae, lemon-yellow
Iris 'Katherine Hodgkin', creamy, blue and yellow-veined
Narcissus bulbocodium 'Nylon', white, scented

PERENNIALS

Helleborus abshasicus, plum
H. argutifolius (syn. *H. corsicus*), icy green E
H. atrorubens, dark red
H. foetidus, soft green E
H. orientalis, cream; pink; ruby; purple E
H. viridis, strong green
Primula wanda 'Tawny Port'
Pulmononaria rubra, coral-pink

TREES

Acer griseum (for red peeling bark)
Arbutus unedo (for red bark; also autumn fruit) E
Betula nigra (for shaggy rufous bark)
Pinus bungeana (for patterned bark) E
Prunus subhirtella autumnalis (for flowers)

PLANT INDEX

Explanation of plant lists 16